Nature's WORST Parents

# MEAN Mammals

Alix Wood

Gareth Stevens PUBLISHING

**Please visit our website, www.garethstevens.com. For a free color catalog of all our high-quality books, call toll free 1-800-542-2595 or fax 1-877-542-2596.**

**Cataloging-in-Publication Data**
Names: Wood, Alix.
Title: Mean mammals / Alix Wood.
Description: Buffalo, NY : Gareth Stevens Publishing, 2027. | Series: Nature's worst parents | Includes glossary and index.
Identifiers: ISBN 9781482477689 (pbk.) | ISBN 9781482477696 (library bound) | ISBN 9781482477702 (ebook)
Subjects: LCSH: Mammals--Juvenile literature.
Classification: LCC QL706.2 W65 2027 | DDC 599--dc23

Published in 2027 by
**Gareth Stevens Publishing**
2544 Clinton St.
Buffalo, NY 14224



Designed and written by Alix Wood

Picture Credits: all illustrations © Alix Wood;

Photo credits — cover, except top right, 5 bottom, 6, 7, 8, 9, 10, 12, 16, 17, 20, 21, 24, 26, 28, 29, 30, 31 © AdobeStock Images; cover top right, 18 © 3268 Zauber/Creative Commons; 5 middle © Oncewerecolours/Creative Commons; 14 bottom © Talks Presenters09/Creative Commons; 15 © Cathy Withers-Clarke/AdobeStock Images; 19 © Jeremiah's CPs/Creative Commons; 23 © Johannes Oehl/AdobeStock Images



Printed in China
CPSIA compliance information: Batch #QS27GS: For further information contact Gareth Stevens at 1-800-542-2595.

# Contents

# WHAT ARE MAMMALS?

You are a mammal! So are rats, dogs, llamas, bats, and whales! That's a lot of VERY different animals. So, why are we all in the same group? What is a mammal?

**Mammals breathe air.**

**Mammals have fur or hair at some point in their life.**

**A mammal's body temperature stays the same, no matter how hot or cold the weather is.**

**The females produce milk to feed their babies.**

Bats, whales, and you have a lot in common!

Because mammals stick around to feed their babies their milk, most mammals are pretty good parents.

a calf drinking its mom's milk

But some mammal parents are not very good. For instance, a male chimpanzee may kill a baby chimp if they don't think they are its father.

***Mammals CAN be great parents, but they also do some pretty mean things!***

# Giant Pandas

Giant pandas are lazy. Panda dads don't take care of their babies at all. Panda moms can be pretty good parents—unless they have more than one baby!

Pandas eat bamboo.

Around half of all panda births are twins. But a panda mom can't be bothered with raising two cubs. So she just ignores the weaker one.

When pandas are kept in wildlife parks, their keepers secretly swap any twin cubs each day. This way, both cubs get fed, and mom just has to mother one at a time.

## Why Do They Do That?

Bamboo doesn't have many **nutrients.** Pandas have to eat almost half their body weight in bamboo every single day. It takes them around 14 hours of chewing! So moms can't usually make enough milk for two cubs. One strong cub is probably better than two weak ones.

Their poor diet is also why giant pandas don't have much energy.

The lazy pandas often roll from place to place, probably because rolling takes less energy than walking.

## WHAT?

Giant panda cubs eat their mom's poop. Eating the **bacteria** in poop helps the cubs' stomachs prepare to eat the tough bamboo stalks. Luckily, adult pandas poop around 40 times a day, so there is plenty to go around!

# Lions

Lionesses are great moms, most of the time. They keep their cubs safe and feed them with their milk. Lionesses teach the cubs to hunt too. A lioness may even feed another mom's cubs or adopt an **abandoned** cub.

WHAT?

If any cubs are weak or sick, or there is not enough food to go around, a lioness may abandon her cubs. Moms often abandon a single cub too. Why? While her body is producing milk, she can't have more cubs. If she stops feeding that one cub, she can go on to have a bigger **litter** of cubs that year.

Scientists believe around one quarter of cubs are killed or abandoned by their mom and dad!

The fierce male lion protects the cubs, unless the cubs aren't his.

# IF ANY CUBS AREN'T MINE, I KILL THEM!

When a new male lion takes over a group of lions, he usually kills all the cubs.

The female will try to hide or defend the cubs. She may manage to protect older cubs, who are about to leave the group.

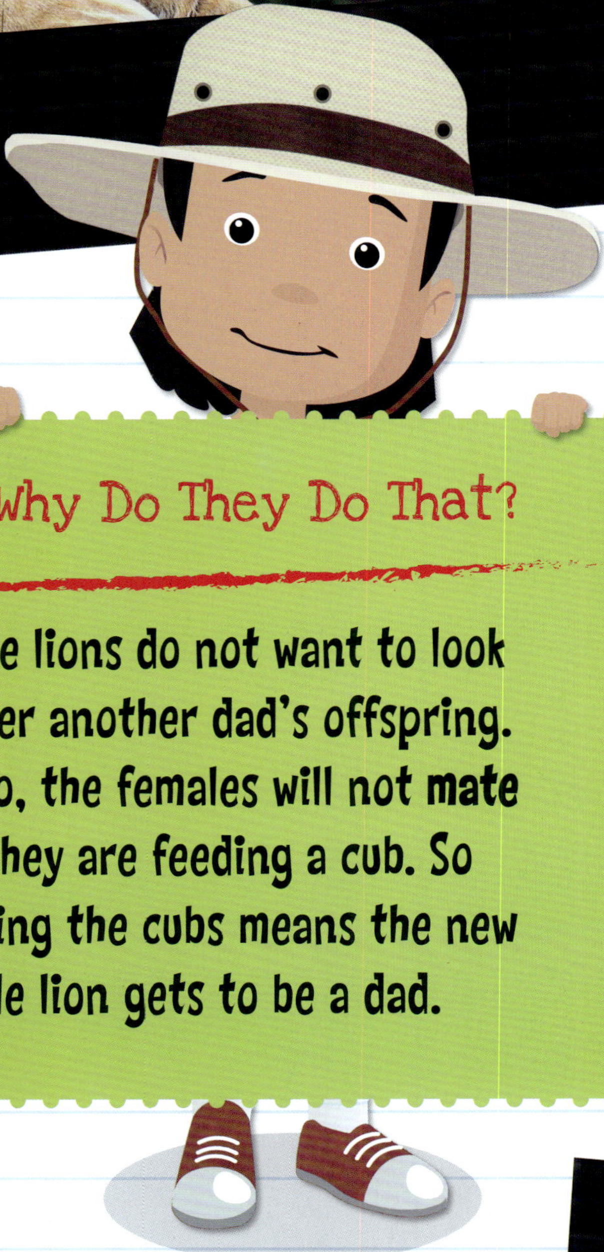

## Why Do They Do That?

**Male lions do not want to look after another dad's offspring. Also, the females will not mate if they are feeding a cub. So killing the cubs means the new male lion gets to be a dad.**

# Giraffes

Giraffes are the tallest land mammal. At around 18 feet (5.5 m), their legs are taller than a tall man! So giraffe moms lie down to have their babies, right? Nope, they stand up!

## WHAT?

It gets worse! After the birth, the mom kicks her baby to make it stand up. Why? Lions, hyenas, leopards, and wild dogs hunt baby giraffes. To stay safe, it needs to be able to stand and run quickly.

Newborn giraffes come out front legs and head first. They fly through the air like a superhero, until they crash to the ground!

**Thanks to mom's friendly kicking, baby giraffes can stand in minutes and run just 10 hours later.**

## Why Do They Do That?

**Giving birth lying down can damage the baby's long neck. The fall helps the baby giraffe burst out of its birth sac. It also shocks the baby into taking its first breath.**

# Hedgehogs

Some animals survive the cold winter by sleeping through it. This is known as **hibernation**. Cute, spiky hedgehogs hibernate during the cold winter months.

During hibernation, hedgehogs don't eat or drink.

MY FALL BABIES WON'T SURVIVE!

Hedgehogs must eat well before hibernation to store enough body fat. Fall babies don't get time to eat enough.

## Why Do They Do That?

Hedgehogs usually have their babies, known as hoglets, in the spring and summer. That gives them time to eat enough to survive hibernation. But sometimes they accidentally have a second batch of hoglets in the fall.

## WHAT?

A hedgehog mom may abandon her babies, or even eat them, if her nest is disturbed.

When mom is tired of feeding her hoglets, she lies down flat with her legs out.

Hungry hoglets sometimes have to dig under her to reach the milk!

# Zebras

When a new male zebra takes over a herd, it sometimes kills the baby zebras. Just like male lions, zebra stallions do not want to bring up another zebra's babies.

**Male zebras have been known to kill their own sons too. Killing the males gets rid of the competition for females.**

Female zebras won't mate with a new male stallion if they are feeding a foal with their milk. If the stallion kills the foals, then the females will be ready to mate.

# WHAT?

Female zebras, called mares, have been known to kill their own offspring too. This happens most often when the zebras live in captivity, such as in zoos.

Zebra moms keep their newborn foals apart from the rest of the herd for a few days. This lets the babies learn to recognize their mom among the sea of stripes!

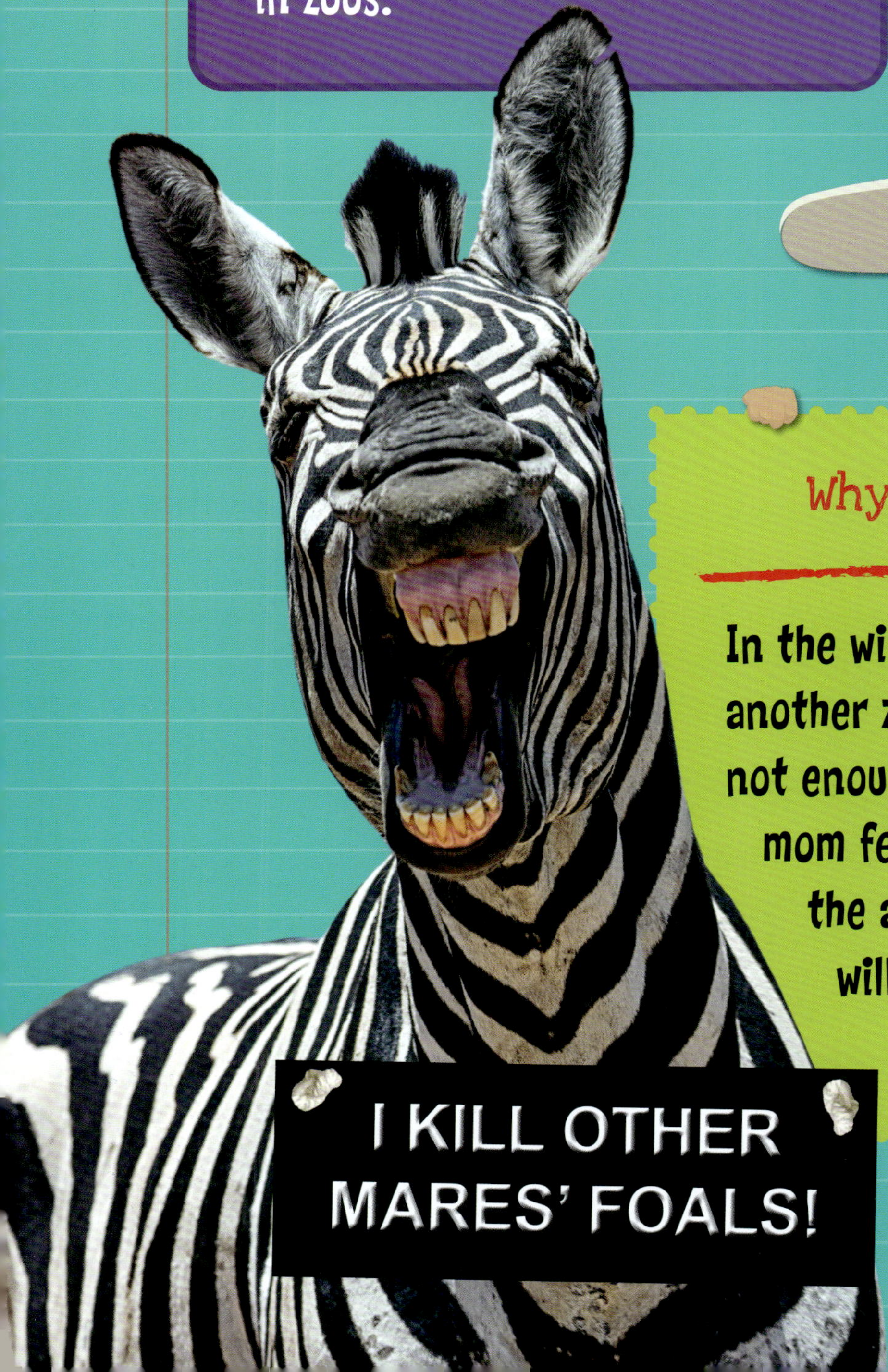

## Why Do They Do That?

In the wild, a zebra mom may kill another zebra's foal if there is not enough food to go around. The mom fears the other foal may eat the available food and there will be none left for her foal.

# Rhesus Monkeys

Some types of monkeys can be pretty mean to their babies. But the rhesus monkey would probably win top prize for being the WORST!

**Rhesus monkey moms have been seen dangling their babies by the leg from high up in the trees.**

## WHAT?

**The monkey moms have been seen sitting or standing on on their babies, or dragging them along by the arm or leg. They sometimes use their hands to shove a baby into the ground too.**

## Why Do They Do That?

Kids can be pretty annoying, but that's no excuse for bad parenting. Scientists think that most bad monkey moms were treated badly when they were babies, so that's how they think parents should behave.

a baby rhesus monkey pulling mom's fur

**Monkeys spend a lot of time grooming each other. Maybe this annoying monkey is just learning how?**

Mom's who are still caring for an older daughter often quickly stop caring for a new baby. Scientists think this is because they expect their daughter to look after the infant for them.

# Treeshrews

High up in a hole in a tree, a treeshrew makes her nest. She lines the hollow with soft, dry leaves.

Now the nest is ready for her babies when they are born.

I DON'T LIVE WITH THE KIDS!

So far, so cute. Then, she leaves her babies all alone in their nest, and heads back to her nest!

A treeshrew mom only visits the nest every few days to feed her babies. She stays for a few minutes and leaves again!

## Why Do They Do That?

Living in a separate nest may seem uncaring, but there is a good reason. Treeshrews are quite smelly! Her smell might lead **predators** to her babies. The mother varies her route, too, to keep predators from following her **scent** trail.

## WHAT?

Treeshrews and pitcher plants have a strange relationship! The shrews feed on a sweet substance on the plant's lid. In return, they poop into the pitcher, which acts as food for the plant.

# Hamsters

Wild hamsters raise their babies in a nest in their underground burrow. They line the nest with soft material such as grass, wool, and leaves.

MY BABIES MAY BE LUNCH!

A hamster may give birth to as many as 20 tiny babies at once. If the nest is overcrowded, hamsters have a gruesome solution!

Hamsters may kill and eat some of their babies if their nest is too full. The remaining babies then have a healthier space to live in.

grass nest

Hamsters also kill any babies that seem sick. This keeps any disease from spreading to the other babies.

## Why Do They Do That?

A hamster will eat her babies if she feels stressed or can't take care of them. She may eat them if the nest is threatened by a predator too. She kills them believing a quick death is better for them than suffering.

## WHAT?

**Hamsters can become sick if they only eat corn. This diet lacks a vitamin that hamsters need. This illness affects their brains, making them more likely to eat their babies.**

A hamster mom leaves her scent on her babies. The scent helps her recognize them. If she smells a new scent on her babies, she may kill them.

# Sloths

Sloths are not the most energetic animals. They spend their time just hanging around in trees.

Sloth moms even have their babies while hanging from the branches. They usually move to the bottom of the tree. At least then, when the baby drops out, it doesn't fall too far! Thanks, mom!

## WHAT?

**If the baby sloth's umbilical cord doesn't break as it falls, its first experience of the world can be like a crazy bungee jump!**

The baby sloth crawls up onto its mom's chest and clings to her fur. It clings on for the next six months, drinking mom's milk and learning which leaves are safe to eat. Sometimes, a baby sloth falls off. It may get injured or abandoned.

## Why Do They Do That?

Sloths feel safer in the trees. If a baby falls, the mother may not feel safe to leave the trees to rescue it.

HANG ON TIGHT, BABY!

Sloths occasionally have twins. A sloth mom would struggle to have the energy to look after two babies. There is only really room for one baby to hang on too. The weakest twin is usually left behind.

# Pigs

Female pigs are known as sows. Sows are much larger than their newborn piglets. Many piglets are killed by their own mom rolling over and crushing them! On cold days, piglets snuggle up close to mom, which is risky!

**A sow may crush her piglets on purpose. She can only feed 14 of them but can have litters of 20.**

Some farmers put heat lamps in the pig pen, away from the sow. The piglets can safely keep warm underneath them.

## Why Do They Do That?

First-time moms, and sows who haven't watched other pigs look after piglets, are more likely to crush their babies. Sows that are given time and space to bond with their piglets are less likely to crush them.

Weak piglets can't get out of the way quick enough, so the strongest and fastest will survive!

## WHAT?

A pig mom sometimes eats a piglet soon after it is born. They may do this if they think the piglet is too weak to survive.

# Black Bears

Black bear moms usually have two or three cubs. The cubs are born in winter in the bear's den. They are helpless at birth and need a lot of care. Mom keeps them warm, clean, and fed. The male bears don't help raise the cubs.

**Mother bears teach their cubs how to climb, find food, and avoid danger. BUT—they're not perfect!**

## WHAT?

If a black bear has just one cub, she will often abandon it or kill it.

### Why Do They Do That?

The mom may decide it is not worthwhile to spend the whole year bringing up just one cub. If she abandons or kills that cub, she can go on to have two or three more cubs that year.

Even with two or three cubs, in the spring the mom starts to get tired of caring for them. She will drive them away, so she is ready to mate and have more cubs the next year.

# Hippos

Crocodiles, hyenas, leopards, and lions all hunt baby hippos. But most hippopotamus babies are actually killed by other hippos, including their own parents!

Female hippos give birth away from the group. They return once their calf has bonded with them and is able to run from danger. They know male hippos may harm a young hippo.

Hippos kill around 500 people each year too!

## WHAT?

Baby hippos often get killed accidentally when adult hippos fight each other. An adult hippo's weight, speed, and huge teeth are very dangerous.

A hippo can weigh as much as three small cars. They have razor-sharp long teeth and a bite force that can crush bones.

Hippos can run at 19 miles (30 km) per hour!

### Why Do They Do That?

Hippos need to guard their food, water, and territory. They will attack if they feel threatened.

# Glossary

**abandoned** To leave a place, person, or thing, usually forever.

**bacteria** Very tiny living organisms with only one cell, including some that can cause disease.

**birth sac** A thin bubble of fluid that protects a developing baby.

**hibernation** A long, deep nap that some animals take over winter when it's cold and there's not much food to eat.

**litter** A group of baby animals that were born at the same time to the same mother.

**mate** Two animals coming together to make babies.

**nutrients** Substances found in food that help living things stay healthy and grow.

**predators** Animals that hunt, kill, and eat other animals for food.

**scent** A particular smell that an animal or human gives off.

**umbilical cord** The long tube that runs between a mom and her unborn baby. It carries oxygen and nutrients to the baby and waste away from the baby.

# Index